Saving Your

RETIREMENT

Will I Have Enough?

Douglas L. Dombey

ARCHWAY
PUBLISHING

Archway Publishing books may be ordered through booksellers or by contacting:

Archway Publishing
1663 Liberty Drive
Bloomington, IN 47403
www.archwaypublishing.com
1 (888) 242-5904

Because of the dynamic nature of the Internet, any web addresses or
links contained in this book may have changed since publication and
may no longer be valid. The views expressed in this work are solely those
of the author and do not necessarily reflect the views of the publisher,
and the publisher hereby disclaims any responsibility for them.

Any people depicted in stock imagery provided by Thinkstock are models,
and such images are being used for illustrative purposes only.
Certain stock imagery © Thinkstock.

ISBN: 978-1-4808-4261-8 (sc)
ISBN: 978-1-4808-4262-5 (e)

Library of Congress Control Number: 2017900592

Print information available on the last page.

Archway Publishing rev. date: 06/05/2017

ACKNOWLEDGEMENTS

Throughout my career I have always been surrounded and supported by great people. I know that I would not be where I am today without their unwavering support. That being said I must mention those that provided such support on this project.

Diane Allison – you are not only an awesome sister but also a tremendous artist. Thank you for the cover design.

Martha Fosdick – always the supportive and faithful friend. Thank you for being an honest and diligent editor.

Sharon Parrish – it has been quite the journey. Thanks for your loyalty and always being willing to go the extra mile.

Skip – thanks for being the definition of a true friend and challenging me on my theories and concepts throughout this project.

The love of my life Mary – thank you for being the best mom and wife a man could desire. You provide the spiritual support I need to carry on. I love you.

NOTE TO READERS

This book is not intended to provide tax or investment advice. Nor is it promoting any specific company or product. As always you should consult a professional before implementing any concept or strategy.

It is my hope that this book will help you to create a healthier retirement plan.

CONTENTS

Introduction xi

1 Tax Rates 1

2 Portfolio Turnover 5

3 The Tax Effect 8

4 Qualified Plans 12

5 The Market 17

6 Sequence of Returns 21

7 Non-Correlated Assets 34

8 Fees vs. Taxes 41

9 Doing the Math 47

10 How Does an Equity-Indexed Life Insurance
    Policy Work? 57

11 Conclusion 64

About the Author 67

INTRODUCTION

Having been in the financial-planning business since 1982, I have found it very interesting to see all the different products, concepts, and philosophies come and go. But along the way, I have noticed how opinions or ideas about investing have somehow become fact, if not gospel, even if the underlying assumptions are not as clear-cut or accurate as many believe.

I would like to take a closer look at some of those so-called facts to see whether they are true. As I will explain in the following pages, their veracity can have significant consequences for your retirement. For example, return on investment is a critical factor in your retirement strategy. Yet a singular focus on the rate of return may obscure the importance of dealing with actual losses in your portfolio. So for that reason, vehicles that traditionally have been thought to provide poor investment returns may in fact be the most efficient ones in our retirement years. Why don't more people know about this?

Traditionally, fees (commissions, management fees, wrap fees, trade fees, etc.) have been considered the major factor in wealth accumulation. Fees are important, but they may not be the greatest deterrent to wealth accumulation. Taxes may be more important.

I will investigate some of the tenets of traditional financial planning to see where they are true and where they are not. Issues I examine include the effect of taxes on retirement, the philosophy of qualified plans, the risk of market instability, and, finally, the effect of negative returns early in retirement.

Then we will do the math to show viable solutions to these challenges using a tax-free investment strategy that many financial planners overlook.

1

TAX RATES

Before we can understand the opportunity that tax-free investments bring, we must study how taxes affect our investments. I begin with historical income tax rates. The current environment is relatively tax friendly. However, going back several decades reveals significantly higher tax rates. (See the following chart.) So let us begin by examining the year 1981. The federal marginal tax rates for married filing jointly with $215,400 of income or greater was 70 percent. If you had $109,000 of income, your marginal rate was 64 percent. Looking at today's economy, the national debt, and the structure of the federal government, I believe income taxes are very likely to go up in the future.

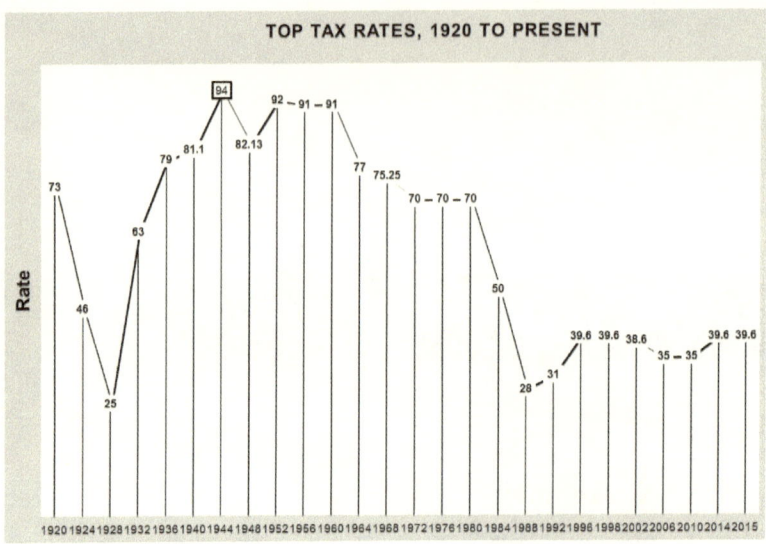

TOP TAX RATES, 1920 TO PRESENT

When analyzing how tax rates have declined over the years, we must recognize that many tax deductions (consumer interest, accelerated depreciation on real estate, etc.) have been eliminated, while new phase outs on deductions such as mortgage interest deductions have been introduced. Actual marginal rates have gone down; however the actual income tax paid has likely gone up.

You might ask, "When looking at our investments, why should we be so concerned about ordinary income tax rates? Don't we receive long-term capital gain treatment on our investments?" That may or may not be true because the preponderance of money people have is in their qualified plans, such as 401(k)s, or in their homes. Yes, profits on their homes up to $250,000 if they are single or $500,000 if married are tax-free. And everything above that is taxed as a long-term capital gain if they owned the home for twelve months or more. However, I do not consider home equity an actual retirement asset. Unless retirees sell their houses and move into tents, they will be living in houses somewhere. As long as that money is tied up in their houses, they cannot use it for retirement income without adding risk via home equity loans or reverse mortgages. So let's take that off the table for the moment. Qualified plan (a 401(k), for example) money is considered ordinary income and taxed as such.

NOTES

2

PORTFOLIO TURNOVER

You might say, "I have a lot of other nonqualified (non - 401(k), IRA, etc.) investments in the market, such as mutual funds, on which I am going to be taxed at long-term capital gain rates." However, what is the tax cost of those investments, and what does the portfolio turnover (the percentage of assets purchased and sold typically measured over a twelve-month period) look like? If we go onto the website of investment research firm Morningstar's fund-screening tool, we find that the average annual portfolio turnover for domestic stock funds is 95 percent, and the average portfolio turnover for international stock funds is 80 percent. What that says is the bulk of these portfolio returns are short-term capital gains, which are taxed as ordinary income.

A perfect example of this scenario was demonstrated in the great plunge the market took in 2008. Many people, including many of you, lost money in that market, yet they still had to pay income tax on the portfolio turnover. The reason is there were short-term (taxed as ordinary income) and long-term capital gains created by the sale of assets as investors liquidated their mutual funds, stocks, bonds, and managed money accounts. Some of the assets that were sold were profitable (worth more than they paid for them), so taxes were paid despite the overall decline in their portfolios. It is an odd circumstance, but because it does happen, we need to factor that possibility into our planning. If someone is going to pay income tax on those investments, then what effect does that have?

3

THE TAX EFFECT

An Associated Press article reported that Lipper Inc. (an investment research firm) performed a study on the tax period between the years 2000 and 2009 with very interesting results. The study found that stock mutual funds held in taxable accounts gave up nearly 1 percent of their investment returns to taxes each year from 2000 to 2009. In comparison during that decade, the Standard & Poor's index averaged a 1 percent loss annually, not counting that 1 percent hit from taxes. Consequently, even though investors already had a 1 percent loss to the market, there was another 1 percent lost to taxes, so investors actually had a 2 percent loss in a market that was down 1 percent. Interestingly, Lipper Inc. went on to look at the late 1990s. During that period, there was a big rally in the market, and income taxes actually shaved nearly three points from returns. In other words, if a fund published that investors made a 10 percent return, the net on that return after taxes would have only been 7 percent. From a long-term perspective, taxes have a dramatic effect on returns.

My clients often say, "I have an exchange-traded fund," or, "I have an index fund, and as a result, they're very tax efficient."

Craig Israelsen, in his March 24, 2015, *Financial Planning.com* article "How Efficient Is that Fund?" looks at the five-year tax efficiency (assuming the funds are sold at the end of that five-year period) of two of the largest ten funds and compares the after-tax performance as calculated by Lipper Inc.

Fund Name	5 Year Annualized Return 2010-2014	After-Tax 5- Year Annualized Return 2010-2014	Tax Efficiency
SPDR S&P 500 ETF Trust	15.31	11.88	0.78
Vanguard Institutional Indexed Fund	15.55	12.55	0.81

First, look at the "Tax Efficiency" column. Tax efficiencies of 1.0 indicate an after-tax return that is the same as a pretax return. A score of 0.5 would indicate that half the gross return was lost to taxes. Examining the SPDR S&P 500 exchange-traded fund over a five-year period, from 2010 to 2014, there was a five-year annualized return of 15.31.

The after-tax, five-year annualized return for that same period was 11.88, giving it a tax efficiency rating of 0.78. What that 0.78 really means is a loss of 3.43 percent of the annualized return to taxes, a significant amount. In the case of a 15 percent return, that means an actual loss of more than 20 percent of our return to taxes. That is expensive when compared to the actual percentage return.

The same is true when looking at the Vanguard Institutional Index Fund. It had a five-year return of 15.42, and the after-tax return was 12.44. That represents a three-point loss! So what does that mean from a dollars and cents perspective?

According to Morningstar's chart "The Tax Bite Is Bigger than You Think," if $1 had been invested in stocks in 1926, that $1, before taxes, would be worth $4,677 in 2013. However, on an after-tax basis (assuming a single taxpayer with a $110,000 income in 2010 dollars adjusted for the Consumer Price Index and applying the appropriate federal income and capital gains tax rates, no state tax), it would be worth $934. So the effect of taxes reduces your retirement nest egg, in this case, by $3,743, which is 80 percent. And if you had invested in bonds over that same period, from 1926 to 2013, your $1 would have grown to $109. However, after tax, it would only be worth $18. You can see the dramatic effect taxes have on your retirement. What do we take away from this? Be very, very aware of the tax efficiency of the funds and the types of accounts you invest in. By examining how taxes effect your taxable investments, you begin to appreciate the opportunity that tax-favored investments bring to a well-rounded retirement portfolio.

A lot of people might think the best solution to the tax problem lies with qualified plans, which offer tax-deferred growth. However, as you will see, there are some problematic assumptions made that could put your retirement at risk.

NOTES

4

QUALIFIED PLANS

I want to talk about qualified plans by examining how they work, what they do compared to other strategies, and how they mesh with some other opportunities in the financial-planning process.

First, please understand that I am not against qualified plans; 401(k)s, defined benefit pension plans, profit-sharing plans, and IRAs are great vehicles. They are good ways to accumulate wealth and can definitely create a forced investment for employees as well as employers. It certainly gives them opportunities to create wealth. That said, let's explore more closely the philosophy of a qualified plan.

First, we take a portion of the money we currently have and put it into, say, a 401(k) plan, thereby reducing our taxable income. Each of those dollars is going to grow with no tax whatsoever, so the fund continues to grow until retirement. At retirement, we have the opportunity to access that money for retirement income. However, it is then 100 percent taxable.

Traditional wisdom is that you are taking a tax deduction today, so that it may grow tax deferred, letting that whole dollar go to work now, and on retirement, you will be in a lower income tax bracket. That philosophy certainly made sense in 1980, when the first 401(k) was put in place, and the top tax rate was 70 percent.

However, does it make sense today? Few believe that tax rates, or effective taxes, will go down in the future, especially when considering the growing national debt. Most everyone I talk with—CPAs, attorneys, investment advisers, financial planners, and clients—concur that the effective tax rate likely will be higher in the future. The following graph shows the relationship between income tax rates and the national debt. For the national debt to go down, there will have to be an increase in income tax rates. If that is true, does it make sense to take a tax deduction now, in what may be the lowest income tax bracket of our lifetimes? Does it make sense to defer all that tax on both the principal and the interest until retirement so that we can pay tax on both the principal and interest at a higher income tax rate? Instead, would it not be more prudent to pay tax on those dollars today and never pay tax again on the principal or interest earned on that account?

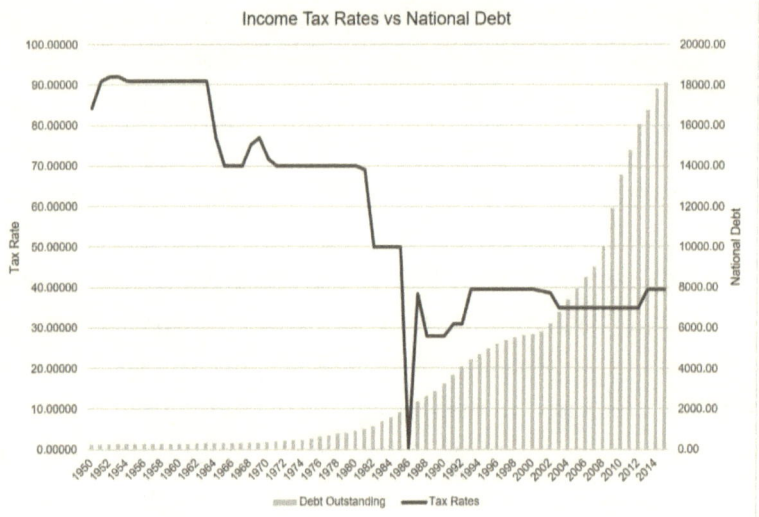

You need to look at this tax question from the perspective of retirement years. When you are contributing to a pension plan, 401(k), or profit-sharing plan, you are enjoying a 100 percent tax deduction. But in retirement, you do not have an income stream other than savings, pension accounts, Social Security, and the other wealth you accumulated to continue living in the same manner you did during your working years. Not only do you have to pay taxes on the taxable retirement income, you may also lose deductions, such as mortgage interest, dependent deductions, or business expenses. Consequently, you will be paying taxes from what you have saved through the years at a potentially higher rate.

To illustrate, you may have built a $1 million retirement fund, but it is not worth $1 million because you will pay tax on that income stream when you are not working. In other words, you have to take it out of your savings.

On the other hand, by doing the math, if you pay taxes now, during your working lifetime when there is more cash flow, and if you do not have to pay tax on your retirement income stream, you will not have to accumulate as much money. For example, if you accumulated $1 million in a 401(k) and took a distribution of 7 percent (or $70,000)—all of which is taxable—you would net $52,500, assuming a 25 percent tax rate. However, if the distribution were tax-free, you would only have to accumulate $750,000 to net $52,500, assuming a 7 percent distribution. If you do accumulate the same amount of money in the tax-free account as you did in a qualified plan, you will have a much richer retirement income because you do not pay any tax.

So the question becomes "Do I want to pay taxes during my working lifetime when I have income, lock in the current tax rate, and not be subject to future tax increases, or do I want to pay taxes out of my retirement savings and be subject to unknown, probably increasing tax rates, which means I will have to accumulate more wealth to meet my needs?"

Not only are all qualified plan distributions taxable, but as I will explain, the underlying investment—and thus your retirement income stream—is exposed to market instability and sequence of return risk (receiving a negative return early in retirement).

NOTES

5

THE MARKET

When people retire, many have a common concern, especially when they see the stock market fluctuate. They wonder if that instability will erode their retirement savings. It is a reasonable concern, given how the average lifespan is increasing, as well as many people's increasing dependency on personal savings rather than government or employer-sponsored retirement benefits and since bonds, with their low interest rates, do not offer a viable alternative. The *Wall Street Journal* echoed these concerns when it highlighted what is called "sequence of returns." This has to do with how market losses, particularly in early retirement, can erode a portfolio and dramatically affect long-term retirement funds. (Sequence of returns will be examined in chapter 6.)

This chapter focuses on the realities of the stock market itself. We continue to examine investment philosophy and the assumptions that support it.

There is a common feeling that the stock market has been volatile and experienced a lot of down years recently. To assess the actual risk, let's review the Standard & Poor's 500 (S&P 500) history to see how income is affected not only by down markets but also by up markets. The last ten years is a good place to begin.

First, how many down years have there been in the last ten years? And in the ten years previous to that, how many down years do you think there were, and in the ten years prior? Most believe the market has been down almost as much as it has been up. I sense they are responding not just to what has happened in the actual market but how the overall economy feels to them.

It is very interesting to compare their responses to the S&P 500. Starting with the years 2005 to 2014, there has been one down year in the market. In the prior ten years, 1995 to 2004, there have been three down years. And from 1985 to 1994, there was one down year.

Let's broaden the scale and look at the up years and down years over a longer period. For each decade since the Great Depression, the following shows what percentage of the years the S&P 500 has **increased** in value.

1930s	40 percent	Great Depression
1940s	70 percent	World War II
1950s	80 percent	
1960s	70 percent	
1970s	70 percent	High inflation/interest rates
1980s	90 percent	
1990s	90 percent	Dot com bubble

2000–2009   60 percent   Dot-com bust, 9/11, and the
                               Great Recession
2010–2015   100 percent

Considering what the market has done historically, it has been up
more often than not. In fact, there has never been a twenty-year
period when the S&P 500 has been down more than 50 percent
of the time. However, in recent years, there has been significant
volatility. Between 2000 and 2009, the market was up only 60
percent of the time. This is important because it means that
with four down years in one decade, people needed downside
protection for their portfolios. If you had retired in 2000, you
would have had negative returns of 9.11 percent, 11.89 percent,
and 22.1 percent for the first three years of your retirement. This
would be followed by gains of 28.6 percent, 10.88 percent, 4.91
percent, 15.79 percent, and 5.49 percent for the next five years.
Then in 2008, you would have a negative of 37 percent followed
by a positive yield of 26.46 percent in 2009.

Given the early loss of funds accumulated up to that point, that
sequence of returns would have had a dramatic effect on your
ability to retire effectively. By examining the sequence of returns
more closely in the next chapter, we will think about the market
in more specific terms. Yes, the market is up more than down,
but *when* that downside comes has a critical impact on retirement
cash flow. Since no one has a crystal ball, it is important to plan
for the worst in order to be able to retire effectively in case of a
significant downturn. And if you are fortunate to hit the best-case
scenario, you will have an even more fruitful retirement.

NOTES

6

SEQUENCE OF RETURNS

With the potential for market losses during the early years of your retirement and the consequent erosion of long-term retirement funds, what can be done during your working years to offer more protection?

The more common questions everyone asks are, "Do I have enough?" "Will I outlive my funds?" However, the question ought to be, "Can I take enough money out of my retirement fund to maintain my lifestyle?"

In a *USA Today* article on July 26, 2015, Dan Caplinger from The Motley Fool indicated the biggest threat to your retirement number is the sequence of returns.

> "In doing research on the retirement-number question, many experts have noticed that the most difficult situations retirees face occur when a major market correction occurs soon after a

person retires. Even when overall average annual returns over the long run are similar, a retiree who suffers poor performance early in retirement has a much harder time preserving his assets than one who's fortunate enough to avoid bad markets until later on. Indeed, in some cases, even a retiree who has a higher average annual return in retirement still ends up worse off if the worst years come early on. Experts call this problem sequence-of-return risk, and the problem stems from the fact that retirees need to take withdrawals from their savings in order to cover their living expenses in retirement. In simplest terms, bad performance early in retirement forces you to "sell low" by liquidating investments at fire-sale prices to cover your required withdrawals. If poor initial returns last long enough, then you won't have enough money to enjoy the full benefit of any future rebound in the financial markets".

This is why pundits suggest that a retiree take a maximum of a 4 percent retirement distribution to be safe. The common theme is that if you have a million dollars and you take out 4 percent each year, giving you $40,000 per year of income, this is a safe approach to retirement fund withdrawal.

I find that inadequate for most people; $40,000 is just not enough money to retire on for someone who has accumulated $1 million in retirement savings. The other concern, discussed in the previous chapter, is fluctuation in the stock market. If there is a big loss, particularly early on, how does that impact your portfolio?

With analysis, could you sequence your withdrawals or income differently? First, referring to Figure 1, look at the average return (which is typically used when referring to a historical return of the S&P 500) for the S&P 500 for the twenty-one-year period from 1973 through 1993. It assumes a 7 percent annual withdrawal, which is inflated 1 percent per year. That scenario leaves a balance of $2,134,600 at age eighty-five. Looks pretty good!

S&P 500 / 1973 - 1993 Average Return

Age	401K Balance	7% Pre Tax Withdrawal	Post Withdrawal Balance	Balance	S&P Return
65	$ 500,000	$35,000	$ 465,000	$ 523,637	12.61%
66	$ -	$35,350	$ 488,287	$ 549,859	12.61%
67	$ -	$35,704	$ 514,156	$ 578,991	12.61%
68	$ -	$36,061	$ 542,930	$ 611,394	12.61%
69	$ -	$36,421	$ 574,973	$ 647,477	12.61%
70	$ -	$36,785	$ 610,692	$ 687,700	12.61%
71	$ -	$37,153	$ 650,547	$ 732,580	12.61%
72	$ -	$37,525	$ 695,056	$ 782,702	12.61%
73	$ -	$37,900	$ 744,802	$ 838,722	12.61%
74	$ -	$38,279	$ 800,443	$ 901,379	12.61%
75	$ -	$38,662	$ 862,717	$ 971,506	12.61%
76	$ -	$39,048	$ 932,457	$ 1,050,040	12.61%
77	$ -	$39,439	$1,010,601	$ 1,138,038	12.61%
78	$ -	$39,833	$1,010,207	$ 1,137,594	12.61%
79	$ -	$40,232	$1,097,362	$ 1,235,740	12.61%
80	$ -	$40,634	$1,195,106	$ 1,345,809	12.61%
81	$ -	$41,040	$1,304,768	$ 1,469,300	12.61%
82	$ -	$41,451	$1,427,849	$ 1,607,901	12.61%
83	$ -	$41,865	$1,566,035	$ 1,763,513	12.61%
84	$ -	$42,284	$1,721,229	$ 1,938,276	12.61%
85	$ -	$42,707	$1,895,569	$ 2,134,600	12.61%

Figure 1

Now look at Figure 2, which reflects the same withdrawals. However, it shows the *actual returns*, not the average return, for the same twenty-one-year period. The actual performance has a balance of $222,395 at age eighty-five. That does not leave much room for error. What if you live longer than age eighty-five?

S&P 500 / 1973 - 1993

Age	401K Balance	7% Pre Tax Withdrawal	Post Withdrawal Balance	Balance	S&P Return
65	$ 500,000	$35,000	$ 465,000	$ 396,831	-14.66%
66	$ -	$35,350	$ 361,481	$ 265,797	-26.47%
67	$ -	$35,704	$ 230,093	$ 315,688	37.20%
68	$ -	$36,061	$ 279,628	$ 346,291	23.84%
69	$ -	$36,421	$ 309,870	$ 287,683	-7.16%
70	$ -	$36,785	$ 250,898	$ 267,357	6.56%
71	$ -	$37,153	$ 230,203	$ 272,653	18.44%
72	$ -	$37,525	$ 235,128	$ 311,545	32.50%
73	$ -	$37,900	$ 273,645	$ 260,182	-4.92%
74	$ -	$38,279	$ 221,903	$ 269,723	21.55%
75	$ -	$38,662	$ 231,061	$ 283,188	22.56%
76	$ -	$39,048	$ 244,140	$ 259,447	6.27%
77	$ -	$39,439	$ 220,009	$ 289,817	31.73%
78	$ -	$39,833	$ 249,984	$ 296,656	18.67%
79	$ -	$40,232	$ 256,424	$ 269,887	5.25%
80	$ -	$40,634	$ 229,253	$ 267,332	16.61%
81	$ -	$41,040	$ 226,291	$ 298,003	31.69%
82	$ -	$41,451	$ 256,552	$ 248,574	-3.11%
83	$ -	$41,865	$ 206,709	$ 269,693	30.47%
84	$ -	$42,284	$ 227,409	$ 244,737	7.62%
85	$ -	$42,707	$ 202,031	$ 222,395	10.08%

Figure 2

In figure 3, I reversed the order of the actual historical returns from 1973 to 1993, thus putting the losses at the end of the retirement period instead of the beginning. That sequence of returns leaves you with $2,083,376 at age eighty-five.

S&P 500 / 1973 - 1993 in Reverse Order

Age	401K Balance	7% Pre Tax Withdrawal	Post Withdrawal Balance	Balance	S&P Return
65	$ 500,000	$35,000	$ 465,000	$ 511,872	10.08%
66	$ -	$35,350	$ 476,522	$ 512,833	7.62%
67	$ -	$35,704	$ 477,129	$ 622,511	30.47%
68	$ -	$36,061	$ 586,450	$ 568,212	-3.11%
69	$ -	$36,421	$ 531,791	$ 700,315	31.69%
70	$ -	$36,785	$ 663,530	$ 773,742	16.61%
71	$ -	$37,153	$ 736,589	$ 775,260	5.25%
72	$ -	$37,525	$ 737,735	$ 875,470	18.67%
73	$ -	$37,900	$ 837,570	$ 1,103,331	31.73%
74	$ -	$38,279	$1,065,052	$ 1,131,831	6.27%
75	$ -	$38,662	$1,093,169	$ 1,339,788	22.56%
76	$ -	$39,048	$1,300,739	$ 1,581,049	21.55%
77	$ -	$39,439	$1,541,610	$ 1,465,763	-4.92%
78	$ -	$39,833	$1,425,929	$ 1,889,356	32.50%
79	$ -	$40,232	$1,849,125	$ 2,190,104	18.44%
80	$ -	$40,634	$2,149,470	$ 2,290,475	6.56%
81	$ -	$41,040	$2,249,435	$ 2,088,375	-7.16%
82	$ -	$41,451	$2,046,924	$ 2,534,911	23.84%
83	$ -	$41,865	$2,493,046	$ 3,420,459	37.20%
84	$ -	$42,284	$3,378,175	$ 2,483,972	-26.47%
85	$ -	$42,707	$2,441,266	$ 2,083,376	-14.66%

Figure 3

Figures 4 (average rate of return), 5 (actual rate of return) and 6 (rate of return in reverse order) reflect the most recent timeframe with a negative sequence of returns in the S&P 500 (2000-2016) assuming just a 4 percent withdrawal ($20,000) per year inflated by 1 percent per year.

S&P 500 / 2000 - 2016 Average Return

Age	401K Balance	7% Pre Tax Withdrawal	Post Withdrawal Balance	Balance	S&P Return
65	$ 500,000	$20,000	$ 480,000	$ 498,048	3.76%
66	$ -	$20,200	$ 477,848	$ 495,815	3.76%
67	$ -	$20,402	$ 475,413	$ 493,289	3.76%
68	$ -	$20,606	$ 472,683	$ 490,455	3.76%
69	$ -	$20,812	$ 469,643	$ 487,302	3.76%
70	$ -	$21,020	$ 466,282	$ 483,814	3.76%
71	$ -	$21,230	$ 462,584	$ 479,977	3.76%
72	$ -	$21,443	$ 458,534	$ 475,775	3.76%
73	$ -	$21,657	$ 454,118	$ 471,193	3.76%
74	$ -	$21,874	$ 449,319	$ 466,213	3.76%
75	$ -	$22,092	$ 444,121	$ 460,820	3.76%
76	$ -	$22,313	$ 438,506	$ 454,994	3.76%
78	$ -	$22,537	$ 432,458	$ 448,718	3.76%
79	$ -	$22,762	$ 425,956	$ 441,972	3.76%
80	$ -	$22,989	$ 418,983	$ 434,736	3.76%
81	$ -	$23,219	$ 411,517	$ 426,990	3.76%
82	$ -	$23,452	$ 403,539	$ 418,712	3.76%

Figure 4

S&P 500 / 2000 - 2016

Age	401K Balance	7% Pre Tax Withdrawal	Post Withdrawal Balance	Balance	S&P Return
65	$ 500,000	$20,000	$ 480,000	$ 431,328	-10.14%
66	$ -	$20,200	$ 411,128	$ 357,517	-13.04%
67	$ -	$20,402	$ 337,115	$ 258,331	-23.37%
68	$ -	$20,606	$ 237,725	$ 300,437	26.38%
69	$ -	$20,812	$ 279,625	$ 304,763	8.99%
70	$ -	$21,020	$ 283,743	$ 292,255	3.00%
71	$ -	$21,230	$ 271,025	$ 307,939	13.62%
72	$ -	$21,443	$ 286,496	$ 296,609	3.53%
73	$ -	$21,657	$ 274,952	$ 169,123	-38.49%
74	$ -	$21,874	$ 147,249	$ 181,779	23.45%
75	$ -	$22,092	$ 159,687	$ 180,095	12.78%
76	$ -	$22,313	$ 157,781	$ 157,781	0.00%
78	$ -	$22,537	$ 135,245	$ 153,381	13.41%
79	$ -	$22,762	$ 130,619	$ 161,445	23.60%
80	$ -	$22,989	$ 138,456	$ 154,226	11.39%
81	$ -	$23,219	$ 131,007	$ 130,050	-0.73%
82	$ -	$23,452	$ 106,599	$ 116,768	9.54%

Figure 5

S&P 500 / 2000 - 2016 Reverse Order

Age	401K Balance	7% Pre Tax Withdrawal	Post Withdrawal Balance	Balance	S&P Return
65	$ 500,000	$20,000	$ 480,000	$ 525,792	9.54%
66	$ -	$20,200	$ 505,592	$ 501,901	-0.73%
67	$ -	$20,402	$ 481,499	$ 536,342	11.39%
68	$ -	$20,606	$ 515,736	$ 637,450	23.60%
69	$ -	$20,812	$ 616,638	$ 699,329	13.41%
70	$ -	$21,020	$ 678,308	$ 678,308	0.00%
71	$ -	$21,230	$ 657,078	$ 741,053	12.78%
72	$ -	$21,443	$ 719,610	$ 888,358	23.45%
73	$ -	$21,657	$ 866,701	$ 533,108	-38.49%
74	$ -	$21,874	$ 511,234	$ 529,281	3.53%
75	$ -	$22,092	$ 507,188	$ 576,267	13.62%
76	$ -	$22,313	$ 553,954	$ 570,573	3.00%
78	$ -	$22,537	$ 548,036	$ 597,305	8.99%
79	$ -	$22,762	$ 574,543	$ 726,107	26.38%
80	$ -	$22,989	$ 703,118	$ 538,799	-23.37%
81	$ -	$23,219	$ 515,580	$ 448,348	-13.04%
82	$ -	$23,452	$ 424,897	$ 381,812	-10.14%

Figure 6

These spreadsheets illustrate several things.

1. Average returns bear little resemblance to actual market returns and cannot be relied on when analyzing investment performance.
2. Losses early in your retirement can have a dramatic effect on the success of a retirement plan.
3. Having a plan to mitigate early losses in retirement is critical.

Now comes the interesting part. What if you could adjust for those down years in some way? Would it have a significant impact? What if you could find a non-correlated asset that would provide the after-tax equivalent of the withdrawal from a qualified plan to help mitigate the effect of those down years on your retirement plan?

NOTES

7

NON-CORRELATED ASSETS

Before I answer that, let's make sure you are clear on what a non-correlated asset is and why it matters. A non-correlated asset is one whose value changes independently of the core markets—that is, stocks and bonds. Correlation is typically measured on a scale of −100 to 100. For example, if two assets have a correlation of 50, it means that 50 percent of the time when one asset goes up, the other will go up as well. On the other hand, if two assets have a −50 correlation, 50 percent of the time when one goes up, the other goes down.

Traditionally, real estate, precious metals, private equity, and international stocks would be considered non-correlated investments for US investors. However, since 2008, markets are becoming much more correlated. As an example, since 2008, international stocks have a 90 percent correlation to the US stock market, whereas before it had a negative correlation. With the globalization of companies and markets, packaging of mortgages, real-estate investment trusts, and a 24/7 news cycle, most assets are becoming more correlated. So the answer to what one can invest in that will help protect you from a negative sequence of returns becomes even more important.

What if you funded a $425,000 equity-indexed universal life insurance policy with $20,000 for five years (a significantly lower premium may be paid if paid for a longer period of time) beginning at age forty-five? In other words, if we fund a policy with $20,000 a year for five years, how would that help us in retirement?

The answer is—instead of withdrawing $35,000 from your retirement account each year after a down year, you schedule a $27,000 distribution from the equity-indexed universal life insurance policy, which is tax-free. To repeat, distributions from a properly structured life insurance policy are tax-free. The amount of $27,000 is approximately the equivalent of the net after-tax of $35,000 withdrawn from the qualified plan in the retirement account, assuming a 25 percent tax bracket.

By withdrawing the tax free equivalent of the inflation adjusted $35,000 after each down year from 1973 through 1993, the effect is amazing. Instead of having an ending balance of $222,395 (Figure 2) under the traditional plan, the investment account would have an ending balance of $1,834,305 (Figure 7).

Douglas L. Dombey

S&P 500 / 1973 - 1993 with a Non Correlated Investment

Age	401K Balance	7% Pre Tax Withdrawal	Post Withdrawal Balance	Balance	S&P Return	Life Insurance Tax Free distribution
65	$ 500,000	$35,000	$ 465,000	$ 396,831	-14.66%	
66	$ -	$0	$ 396,831	$ 291,790	-26.47%	$27,000
67	$ -	$0	$ 291,790	$ 400,336	37.20%	$27,000
68	$ -	$36,061	$ 364,275	$ 451,118	23.84%	
69	$ -	$36,421	$ 414,697	$ 385,004	-7.16%	
70	$ -	$0	$ 385,004	$ 410,261	6.56%	$27,589
71	$ -	$37,153	$ 373,108	$ 441,909	18.44%	
72	$ -	$37,525	$ 404,384	$ 535,809	32.50%	
73	$ -	$37,900	$ 497,908	$ 473,411	-4.92%	
74	$ -	$0	$ 473,411	$ 575,431	21.55%	$28,709
75	$ -	$38,662	$ 536,769	$ 657,864	22.56%	
76	$ -	$39,049	$ 618,816	$ 657,616	6.27%	
77	$ -	$39,439	$ 617,782	$ 813,804	31.73%	
78	$ -	$39,833	$ 773,573	$ 917,999	18.67%	
79	$ -	$40,232	$ 877,364	$ 923,426	5.25%	
80	$ -	$40,634	$ 882,386	$ 1,028,950	16.61%	
81	$ -	$41,040	$ 987,499	$ 1,300,437	31.69%	
82	$ -	$41,451	$1,300,437	$ 1,259,994	-3.11%	
83	$ -	$0	$1,218,710	$ 1,590,050	30.47%	$31,399
84	$ -	$41,284	$1,548,354	$ 1,666,338	7.62%	
85	$ -	$41,697	$1,666,338	$ 1,834,305	10.08%	

Figure 7

By investing $20,000 per year for five years, which amounts to a $100,000 investment in a $425,000 life insurance policy, you could have earned, under a historical scenario from 1973 through 1993, an additional $1.6 million in your investment account. This means you could comfortably take a higher withdrawal from your accounts in the retirement plan. In other words, under the above scenario, you can take the 7 percent we spoke of instead of being forced to take the "safe" 4 percent, providing a much better lifestyle in retirement.

It is possible for you to withdraw even more. Under the same scenario, you are able to take out 10 percent, or $50,000, a year from the retirement plan and still have $542,204 remaining at the end of that twenty-one-year period.

Using a non-correlated investment to fund the distribution for the years following a down year in the S&P 500 for the years 2000-2016 (Figure 8) provides a 269% greater year-end balance in 2016 than a plan utilizing only the S&P 500 ($314,774 vs $116,768).

S&P 500 / 2000 - 2016 with Non Correlated Investment

Age	401K Balance	7% Pre Tax Withdrawal	Post Withdrawal Balance	Balance	S&P Return	Life Insurance Tax Free distribution
65	$ 500,000	$20,000	$ 480,000	$ 431,328	-10.14%	
66	$ -	$0	$ 431,328	$ 375,083	-13.04%	$15,150
67	$ -	$0	$ 375,083	$ 287,426	-23.37%	$15,302
68	$ -	$0	$ 287,426	$ 363,249	26.38%	$15,155
69	$ -	$20,812	$ 342,437	$ 373,222	8.99%	
70	$ -	$21,020	$ 352,202	$ 362,768	3.00%	
71	$ -	$21,230	$ 341,538	$ 388,055	13.62%	
72	$ -	$21,443	$ 366,612	$ 379,554	3.53%	
73	$ -	$21,657	$ 357,897	$ 220,142	-38.49%	
74	$ -	$0	$ 220,142	$ 271,766	23.45%	$16,406
75	$ -	$22,092	$ 249,674	$ 281,582	12.78%	
76	$ -	$22,313	$ 259,269	$ 259,269	0.00%	
78	$ -	$22,536	$ 236,733	$ 268,479	13.41%	
79	$ -	$22,761	$ 245,718	$ 303,707	23.60%	
80	$ -	$22,989	$ 280,718	$ 312,692	11.39%	
81	$ -	$23,219	$ 289,473	$ 287,360	-0.73%	
82	$ -	$0	$ 287,360	$ 314,774	9.54%	$17,588

Figure 8

Up-front planning and providing a tax-free source of income for occasional use when the market is down creates a much more secure retirement plan and a significantly higher retirement income.

However, what are the downsides, if any, to using life insurance in this way? One objection frequently heard relates to the cost of life insurance. Let's take a closer look at common perceptions about investments and fees.

NOTES

8

FEES VS. TAXES

The impetus for this book was a conversation about investments I had with a CPA several years ago. He said, "You know, we're always very, very concerned about our clients' investments. And when we look at those, one of the things we always try to make sure is that they're aware of what the fees and costs are in their investment program."

This is a common topic in *Money* magazine and other financial publications. One of the most, probably *the* most, important areas to be aware of and pay attention to in your investments is fees. You should be buying no-load funds, low-load funds, or an exchange-traded fund (ETF) because they are the cheapest ways to buy funds.

There is some validity to that, but as you will see in my ensuing conversation with the CPA, the bigger picture may surprise you. I said to him, "That's interesting. So you just look at fees and expenses."

He said, "Yes. We have people come to us all the time proposing different investment structures that have high fees."

"I understand where you're coming from with this," I replied, "but have you looked at life insurance? How do you look at it as an investment?"

"Oh, no, no, no. We never, ever look at life insurance as an investment. It's strictly a death benefit, and the reason we don't is that the costs are simply too high in a life insurance program."

"You know, that's kind of interesting. Would you mind if I do an analysis as to what life insurance would look like compared to a regular investment so we can compare?

"Oh, well, I can do that. I just look at a life insurance illustration. It's no big deal, and I can do the calculation on my HP and see the rate of return."

"Understood. But when you do that, what tax rate are you taking into account?"

"Well," he said hesitantly, "what do you mean by tax rate?"

"Well, the tax rate that's applied to the regular investment that you're going to compare to the life insurance."

"Uhh, I really didn't put a tax rate on that."

"Okay," I continued. "And what fee structure did you use on that outside investment that you're going to compare to the life insurance program?"

He looked at me for a moment. "Well, I didn't really use one."

I told him I understood. "Now, if you'll indulge me, let's do the math."

At that point, we took a look at an outside investment and agreed to make some reasonable assumptions. The first assumption was that we have to include fees, because unless you are an investor who is going to trade all your own accounts—that is, manage them, buy ETFs, and so on—you will definitely have fees involved. Even if you are that self-directed investor, you will still have fees whether you are buying Vanguard or another low-cost fund.

These could very well be 25 or 50 basis points, but what the CPA and I agreed to was "Let's look at some outside sources such as Morningstar, Motley Fool, and *Forbes* to see what they say about the average fee nationwide." We discovered the average fee is about 1.5 percent.

Now, when we say "average fee," that includes all the internal fees involved with buying whatever product it is. If you are buying a mutual fund, that would be the internal charges, loads, and so on. If you are buying a managed account, the fees also include all the trade fees and management expenses that you are paying inside of those accounts, as well as the wrap fee for your financial planner so that he or she gets paid. In total, we have a wrap fee, internal fee, and trade fee structure of typically about 1.5 percent nationally.

However, in this particular analysis, we used 1 percent. I wanted to be conservative on this even though most investment advisers will tell you that is relatively low. In many cases, it is between 1.5 percent and 2 percent.

"Is 1 percent fair?" I asked the CPA.

"Certainly," he said. "That's very fair."

I said, "The other area we need to examine is taxes. You are going to pay taxes on any outside investment, whether you are investing in a mutual fund, managed money, or any other investment. So what kind of taxes are we looking at in that type of structure?" After some research, we determined that the national turnover rate is almost 90 percent in a mutual fund.

However, I felt it was not fair to use a 90 percent turnover rate, so I suggested we use 50 percent. This assumes we have 50 percent long-term capital gains and 50 percent short-term capital gains. If we look at the current tax structure, that creates a tax rate of approximately 30 percent. But again, I said, "Let's be a little bit conservative and use a 25 percent tax rate."

The fact is that 25 percent is being very conservative because that equates to a long-term capital gain rate, including state taxes. Nevertheless, we put all these assumptions into the calculation and did the outside analysis.

When the CPA saw the numbers comparing life insurance with an outside investment, he was shocked. I will go through those numbers in the next chapter. While fees and expenses always are important, they are a very, very small number relative to the effect *taxes* have on your investments. In fact, our analysis revealed that taxes are the greatest factor that limits growth on investment.

Since taxes, not fees, are the component that negatively impacts investments the most, we must reexamine traditional investment philosophy and the assumptions—or the so-called facts— that support it. The question then becomes how we create an opportunity for tax-free growth or tax-free income. How can we mitigate taxes, which hinder our retirement income?

In the next chapter I expand on the argument that, as a non-correlated asset, life insurance should be an integral part of anyone's retirement planning.

NOTES

9

DOING THE MATH

There are two reasons many people have overlooked life insurance as part of an overall investment strategy. One, they think life insurance is strictly about the death benefit, and two, they assume the costs are too high.

However, as I showed in the previous chapter and demonstrate here in more detail, taxes, not fees, hinder your retirement income the most. A well-planned life insurance program will help mitigate those hindrances by creating tax-free growth and income.

So the question becomes: does a life insurance plan make financial sense *regardless* of the death benefit?

Let's walk step by step through the following spreadsheets to analyze life insurance from an economic perspective. Please note that we will not be giving the actual death benefit of the life insurance any value in the analysis. Instead, this is only a cash-on-cash analysis.

The example in figure 9 is for a male, age forty-five, who is paying $20,000 a year over five years (the premium could be reduced significantly if paid for a longer period of time) for a life insurance policy with a $425,000 death benefit.

Life Insurance					
Year	Age	Annual Premium	Annual Income	Life Insurance Accumulation Value @ 7.50%	Life Insurance Expenses
1	45	20,000	-	16,540	4,727
2	46	20,000	-	34,672	4,390
3	47	20,000	-	54,555	4,014
4	48	20,000	-	76,211	3,742
5	49	20,000	-	99,807	3,440
6	50		-	105,120	2,088
7	51		-	111,037	1,890
8	52		-	117,979	1,332
9	53		-	125,634	1,147
10	54		-	133,894	1,117
11	55		-	144,866	199
12	56		-	156,741	211
13	57		-	169,600	219
14	58		-	183,526	225
15	59		-	198,591	248
16	60		-	214,879	280
17	61		-	232,496	311
18	62		-	251,549	344
19	63		-	272,157	379
20	64		-	294,449	413
21	65		(27,662)	289,662	439
22	66		(27,662)	284,450	464
23	67		(27,662)	278,778	488
24	68		(27,662)	272,604	515
25	69		(27,662)	265,854	572
26	70		(27,662)	256,358	624
27	71		(27,662)	246,144	629
28	72		(27,662)	235,175	619
29	73		(27,662)	223,415	588
30	74		(27,662)	210,829	535
31	75		(27,662)	197,385	452
32	76		(27,662)	182,878	505
33	77		(27,662)	167,220	565
34	78		(27,662)	150,319	631
35	79		(27,662)	132,076	702
36	80		(27,662)	112,377	787
37	81		(27,662)	91,102	882
38	82		(27,662)	68,121	988
39	83		(27,662)	43,293	1,106
40	84		(27,662)	16,466	1,239

Figure 9

Notice the column marked "Life Insurance Accumulation Value." This shows the accumulation value with an assumed interest rate of 7.5 percent.

Another thing to note: as I will explain more fully in the next chapter, there are different accounts in which you can invest within these equity-index life insurance policies. The account selected for this example is with a company that offers 150 percent of the S&P 500, up to a maximum of 11 percent. As you can see, that means if the S&P 500 earned 9 percent, you would get the maximum 11 percent. If, on the other hand, the S&P 500 earned 5 percent, you would receive 7.5percent.

In addition, all the expenses in the life insurance policy are shown. Again, the reason is to reject the claim that life insurance is too expensive and that one should not buy it as an investment to build value on a cash basis. However, by showing what the expenses are compared with a normal outside investment and then doing the math, we can demonstrate what makes more sense.

Starting with the first year of life insurance expenses, you can see how $4,700 is relatively expensive. Then the costs go down, declining to as low as $199 before going back up though at a slower rate.

The next column to review is labeled "Annual Income." This shows $27,662 as the tax-free income stream coming from the policy.

Now, let's consider Figure 10, where we take the money and invest it and make a fair comparison.

Take the Money and Invest It				
Annual Investment	Annual income	Investment Account @ 10.3% Gross* minus Taxes and Fees	Mgmt Fee 1% of acct balance	Tax Expense @ 25% of earnings
20,000	-	21,345	200	515
20,000	-	44,125	413	1,065
20,000	-	68,437	641	1,651
20,000	-	94,385	884	2,277
20,000	-	122,077	1,144	2,945
	-	130,286	1,221	3,143
	-	139,047	1,303	3,355
	-	148,398	1,390	3,580
	-	158,377	1,484	3,821
	-	169,027	1,584	4,078
	-	180,394	1,690	4,352
	-	192,525	1,804	4,645
	-	205,471	1,925	4,957
	-	219,288	2,055	5,291
	-	234,035	2,193	5,646
	-	249,773	2,340	6,026
	-	266,569	2,498	6,431
	-	284,495	2,666	6,864
	-	303,627	2,845	7,325
	-	324,045	3,036	7,818
	(27,662)	316,313	2,964	7,632
	(27,662)	308,062	2,887	7,432
	(27,662)	299,256	2,804	7,220
	(27,662)	289,858	2,716	6,993
	(27,662)	279,828	2,622	6,751
	(27,662)	269,123	2,522	6,493
	(27,662)	257,699	2,415	6,217
	(27,662)	245,506	2,300	5,923
	(27,662)	232,493	2,178	5,609
	(27,662)	218,605	2,048	5,274
	(27,662)	203,784	1,909	4,917
	(27,662)	187,965	1,761	4,535
	(27,662)	171,083	1,603	4,128
	(27,662)	153,066	1,434	3,693
	(27,662)	133,837	1,254	3,229
	(27,662)	113,315	1,062	2,734
	(27,662)	91,412	857	2,205
	(27,662)	68,037	638	1,642
	(27,662)	43,090	404	1,040
	(27,662)	16,466	154	397

Figure 10

We will put $20,000 a year over the same five-year period into an outside investment. Then for that investment—whether mutual funds, managed accounts, individual stocks and bonds, real estate, or other options—we assume a return of 10.3 percent. The reason we show 10.3 percent here compared to 7.5 percent on the other side is that is what it will take for the outside investment to provide the same income stream as the life insurance. Why is that?

There are several assumptions in place because we have to take into account fees, expenses, and taxes. As discussed in the previous chapter, we assumed a 1 percent management fee, which is an all-in management fee that includes wrap fees, internal trade fees, mutual fund costs, and any other expenses related to the investment. Remember, if we based this conservative fee assumption on Forbes, Motley Fool, or Morningstar reports, that fee is more typically a minimum of 1.5 percent on average nationally and can be as high as 2.5 percent.

In addition, we have assumed a 25 percent of earnings tax rate, where all earnings are long-term capital gains and take into account state and federal tax rates.

Realistically, though, the average portfolio turns over at almost a 90 percent rate. Therefore, taxes would be more toward the ordinary income tax bracket instead of the rate for long-term capital gains. That means you would be up in the 30 percent to 40 percent range, but we are going to use the 25 percent rate to stay conservative.

With the 10.3 percent return on the outside investment, the retirement income stream is $27,662 per year, which matches with the $27,662 for the life insurance income stream. Notice they both have $16,000 at age eighty-four.

The important question is why does that happen when one earns 10.3 percent and the other 7.5 percent? To find the answer, we compare the expenses between life insurance versus outside investment programs.

Life Insurance		
Year	Age	Program Expenses
1	45	4,727
2	46	4,390
3	47	4,014
4	48	3,742
5	49	3,440
6	50	2,088
7	51	1,890
8	52	1,332
9	53	1,147
10	54	1,117
11	55	199
12	56	211
13	57	219
14	58	225
15	59	248
16	60	280
17	61	311
18	62	344
19	63	379
20	64	413
21	65	439
22	66	464
23	67	488
24	68	515
25	69	572
26	70	624
27	71	629
28	72	619
29	73	588
30	74	535
31	75	452
32	76	505
33	77	565
34	78	631
35	79	702
36	80	787
37	81	882
38	82	988
39	83	1,106
40	84	1,239
Sub Total(s):		44,046

Life Insurance
Total Expenses
$44,046
40 year annual average
$1,101

Figure 11

		Outside Investment	
Year	Age	Management Fee	Tax Expense
1	45	200	515
2	46	413	1,065
3	47	641	1,651
4	48	884	2,277
5	49	1,144	2,945
6	50	1,221	3,143
7	51	1,303	3,355
8	52	1,390	3,580
9	53	1,484	3,821
10	54	1,584	4,078
11	55	1,690	4,352
12	56	1,804	4,645
13	57	1,925	4,957
14	58	2,055	5,291
15	59	2,193	5,646
16	60	2,340	6,026
17	61	2,498	6,431
18	62	2,666	6,864
19	63	2,845	7,325
20	64	3,036	7,818
21	65	2,964	7,632
22	66	2,887	7,432
23	67	2,804	7,220
24	68	2,716	6,993
25	69	2,622	6,751
26	70	2,522	6,493
27	71	2,415	6,217
28	72	2,300	5,923
29	73	2,178	5,609
30	74	2,048	5,274
31	75	1,909	4,917
32	76	1,761	4,535
33	77	1,603	4,128
34	78	1,434	3,693
35	79	1,254	3,229
36	80	1,062	2,734
37	81	857	2,205
38	82	638	1,642
39	83	404	1,040
40	84	154	397
Sub Total(s):		69,848	179,851

Outside Investments
Total Expenses
$249,700
40 year annual average
$6,242.49

Figure 12

Referring to Figure 11, begin by adding up all the expenses in the life insurance. Remember, there are only policy expenses and no tax on life insurance. Therefore, it grows tax-deferred and can be accessed tax-free via loans. The total cost over the life of the plan is $44,046. This averages to $1,100 per year for forty years.

However, with outside investments, there is a management fee plus the tax expense. As indicated in Figure 12, the management fee is $69,848, which alone is more than what is being charged on the life insurance side. In effect, this means on the life insurance side, overall expenses and management fees are less than 1 percent.

The outside investment is even more expensive when taking into account the taxes that are paid, which amount to $179,851. Fundamentally, the total expenses on the outside investment are $249,700, or an annual average of $6,242.

The conclusions are clear. First, the statement that life insurance is too expensive does not apply when we do the math. Second, it is critical to note that taxes are the greatest deterrent to wealth building. Fees are important, but taxes are the big obstacle in building wealth.

NOTES

10

HOW DOES AN EQUITY-INDEXED LIFE INSURANCE POLICY WORK?

In 2008, those who owned equity-indexed universal life policies did not lose a dime of cash value to the market. They were able to stay invested in the index accounts and did not have to worry about market timing. They were also able to participate in the subsequent run up of the S&P 500 without having to endure its decline and then earn back their lost money just to break even. This is an important consideration in light of the sequence of returns and how that affects your ability to take distributions from your assets for retirement.

The ultimate question becomes: how can an insurance company give you the upside of the S&P 500 (with limitations) and guarantee no loss if it goes down?

The answer is simple; your money is never invested in the S&P 500. Instead, at your request, an insurance company uses the interest earned on your account value to purchase options on the S&P 500.

Let's look at an example. Assume you have an account value of $100,000. The insurance company will offer several options for the investment of those funds, and you may choose among them. We focus on two of those options.

#1. The Fixed Account

This account functions much like a one-year certificate of deposit. The insurance company declares the interest rate it will pay each year, which is guaranteed for one year. Let's assume that rate is 4 percent. So on a $100,000 account balance, you would receive $4,000 of interest this year.

#2. The One-Year Index Account

This account credits you with 100 percent of the growth of the S&P 500 up to a maximum of 12 percent and guarantees that you will never earn less than zero. In other words, you cannot lose money to the market. The way the insurance company guarantees an earnings rate of no less than zero is that it takes the $4,000 of interest earnings they were going to pay you on the fixed account and purchases options on the S&P 500 that provide you with all the earnings of the S&P 500 up to 12 percent. So if the market goes up, you will receive that growth up to 12 percent. If it goes down, you will have only lost your $4,000 of earnings from

the fixed account. Your account value (principal) was never at
risk. The following graph demonstrates the value of mitigating
downside risk.

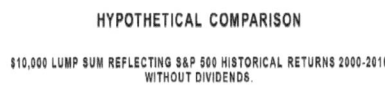

HYPOTHETICAL COMPARISON

$10,000 LUMP SUM REFLECTING S&P 500 HISTORICAL RETURNS 2000-2016
WITHOUT DIVIDENDS.

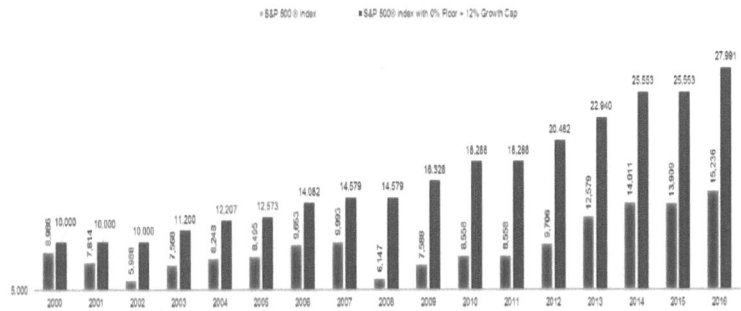

However, it is critical to understand several issues many insurance
agents gloss over.

1. Cap rates: the maximum amount of earnings you can
   receive from the growth of the indexed account; 12 percent
   in our example. These can change based on the price of
   the options and crediting rate on the fixed account. There
   are guarantees in the policy that should be reviewed.

2. Participation rate: the percentage of growth of the indexed
   account you receive; in our example, it was 100 percent.
   Some companies will give you a higher cap rate but only
   give you 80 percent of the growth up to the cap. Others
   will provide a higher participation rate with a lower cap

rate. This is not necessarily bad, but you must know how it works. Please check the guaranteed participation rates.

3. Is the insurance company purchasing the options for the plan from an outside source, such as Goldman Sachs, or hedging internally? If it is hedging internally, you are adding another element of risk to your plan.

4. Do old and new policyholders have the same participation and cap rates as new policy owners? If not, this is an indication of how you will be treated in the future.

The next question is: why is the income from a properly designed life insurance policy tax-free?

Internal Revenue Code Section 72, 7702 and 7702A allow for the following in a properly designed life insurance policy.

1. The cash value grows tax deferred.

2. Withdrawals to basis (the amount you paid into the policy) are tax-free.

3. Distributions above basis are taken as loans and are therefore tax-free.

It is important to understand how the policy loan provisions work. There are two types of loans.

1. *Wash loans.* These loans charge the same rate as they credit on the loaned funds, thus creating a net cost of zero. Confusing? Think of it this way. You use your insurance cash value as collateral for a loan from the insurance company. You place that part of your cash value into an

account that guarantees a 2 percent interest rate, which is your collateral for a loan from the insurance company that will charge you 2 percent. Therefore, you earn 2 percent and are charged 2 percent, so the loan has a net cost of zero.

2. *Variable loan.* The rate charged for these loans changes each year and is generally tied to the Moody's Bond Index, with a cap limiting how high it can go, normally 5 percent to 7 percent. Just like the wash loan, the insurance cash value will be used as collateral for the loan. However, in this case, the funds may be invested in any of the accounts available in the policy. If the earnings are greater than the loan interest, there will be a positive credit to the policy cash values. For example, if the loan rate was 5 percent and the index account earned 7 percent, there would be a positive credit to the cash value for that year. On the other hand, if the loan rate was 5 percent and the indexed account earned zero, there would be a deduction of 5 percent of the loaned amount from the cash value of the policy. This can become a significant number. And if a flat or negative market continues for an extended period, it can have a devastating effect on your policy values.

It is critical to understand what type of loan your policy has and how it works. Variable loans can potentially add significant risk to your planning.

Next, let's enumerate the expenses of a life insurance policy because your cash accumulation is affected by those costs. These expenses cover the acquisition and ongoing costs for the insurance company. These include the underwriting costs, including your physical, production of the policy, marketing, advertising, general overhead (office space, phones, customer service, employee salaries, etc.), insurance agent commissions, and mortality cost (i.e., the actual cost of the death benefit). An insurance company can address these expenses in many ways. Some companies spread them out over a very long period and amortize those acquisition costs. Others will charge it more up front. Still others allow them to be massaged and moved, depending on the clients' particular needs—such as whether they want high cash value early or higher long-term values. Each insurance company has a specific return on investment it strives to achieve, so regardless of the design, policy expenses will meet the insurance companies' return on investment goals.

Therefore, one of the things to be aware of is how these expenses are structured. You should request that your insurance professional provide you with a complete delineation of the expenses. This allows you to compare the insurance policy with outside investments. Then you will see whether those expenses line up with what you are trying to accomplish if you are using a universal life insurance policy as a non-correlated investment asset.

NOTES

11

CONCLUSION

By doing the math, we have demonstrated the following.

1. Taxes are one of the greatest deterrents to wealth accumulation.

2. Average returns bear little resemblance to actual market returns and cannot be relied on when analyzing investment performance.

3. Losses early in your retirement can have a dramatic effect on the success of a retirement plan.

4. Having a plan to mitigate early losses in retirement is critical.

5. The traditional philosophy (or "fact") that life insurance is a poor investment and should be avoided is not true. Life insurance, if designed properly, can have very low expenses over the life of the plan, be an efficient vehicle

for managing taxes, and is the perfect non-correlated asset to offset a negative sequence of return (early losses) in retirement.

Consequently, we should all rethink our investment and retirement strategies to ensure that we are protected from the effect of taxes and losses early in retirement.

Douglas Dombey has served in the financial services industry for more than thirty years. After graduating from Arizona State University, Doug followed in his father's footsteps, entering the financial field in 1982. Three years later, he founded Southwest Financial Group, Inc., specializing in wealth accumulation, conservation, and distribution.

Doug has been the featured speaker at the National Glass Convention, Liberty Life Insurance Company, the Arizona State Bar Association, National Financial Partners Educational Conference, and the Pacific Life University and Symposium. His topics include the dynamics of a successful family business, succession planning, and the uses of life insurance for estate and business planning. Doug taught at the University of Arizona Center for Lifelong Learning as well as the Arizona State University Center for Executive Development.

Doug is a past board member of the United Way Volunteer Bureau, past president of the Christ Lutheran School Board, past president of the Arizona Family Business Alliance, and a founding board member of the Steamboat Springs Winter Sports Club Foundation.

He lives with his wife, Mary, in Steamboat Springs, Colorado, and maintains an office in Phoenix, Arizona.

www.ingramcontent.com/pod-product-compliance
Lightning Source LLC
Chambersburg PA
CBHW022132170526
45157CB00004B/1845

* 9 7 8 1 4 8 0 8 4 2 6 1 8 *